Wayne Gretzky

Terry Barber

SPORTS SERIES

Wayne Gretzky is published by
Grass Roots Press, a division of Literacy Services of Canada Ltd.

PHONE 1–888–303–3213
WEBSITE www.literacyservices.com

ACKNOWLEDGMENTS

We acknowledge the financial support of the Government of Canada through the Book Publishing Industry Development Program (BPIDP) for our publishing activities.

We acknowledge the support of
the Alberta Foundation for the Arts
for our publishing programs.

Editor: Dr. Pat Campbell
Image research: Dr. Pat Campbell
Book design: Lara Minja, Lime Design Inc.

Library and Archives Canada Cataloguing in Publication

Barber, Terry, date
    Wayne Gretzky / Terry Barber.

ISBN 978-1-894593-62-5

        1. Gretzky, Wayne, 1961– . 2. Hockey players—Canada—Biography.
3. Readers for new literates. I. Title.

PE1126.N43B3638 2007   428.6'2
C2007-902782-2

Printed in Canada.

Contents

A hockey scout takes notes.

The Young Hockey Player

You are an NHL hockey scout. You watch young hockey players. You judge their skills. You are good at your job. You can tell if a hockey player will make it in the NHL.

The NHL stands for the National Hockey League. It is the best **league** in the world.

The Young Hockey Player

You watch the young man play. He is just 17 years old. He is a boy playing with men. He is a good player. But can he play in the NHL? The NHL is a hard place to play hockey.

The young man passes the puck.

The Young Hockey Player

The young man scores lots of goals. He passes the puck well. You have seen better skaters. You have seen bigger players. You ask yourself, "Can he can make it in the NHL?"

The young man stands 5′ 11″. He weighs only 165 pounds.

Wayne Gretzky

The Young Hockey Player

No one could have guessed this young man's future. The young man is Wayne Gretzky. Wayne will break every scoring record in the NHL. Wayne will become the greatest hockey player of all time.

Wayne as a young boy.

Early Years

Wayne Gretzky is born in 1961.
Wayne loves hockey from an early age.
He wants to play hockey all the time.
Wayne wants his father to take him
skating all the time. Wayne loves to be
on the ice.

Wayne gets his first pair of skates when he is three.

Walter Gretzky makes a rink.

Early Years

Wayne's father, Walter, knows his son has a special gift. Wayne also works very hard. Walter makes a rink in their back yard. Wayne practices four to five hours a day. Wayne takes his gift and turns it into a **rare** talent.

Wayne has three brothers and one sister. Wayne is the oldest.

Wayne and Walter Gretzky.

Early Years

It is 1966. Wayne is five years old. He asks, "Dad, when can I play on a real team?" Boys can't play on a team until they are ten. These are the rules.

Wayne Gretzky, 1972.

Early Years

Wayne turns six. He tries out for a team. The rules are bent. Wayne gets to play with ten-year-olds. The other players are bigger and stronger. In his youth, Wayne is always the younger, smaller player.

Wayne plays with the Nadrofsky Steelers from 1967 to 1972.

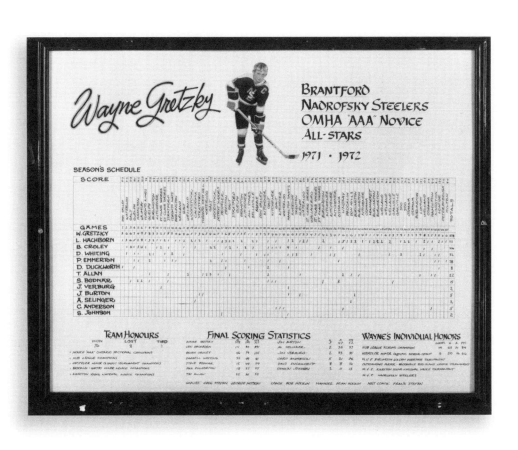

Wayne scores 378 goals in 1971–1972.

Early Years

Wayne's size and age do not matter.
In his first season with the Steelers,
Wayne scores one goal. In his last
season, Wayne scores 378 goals in
82 games. He is only ten years old.

Wayne
moves up to a
Peewee team
in 1972.

The NHL and Number 99

Wayne wears the number 9 when he plays hockey. One year, another player takes the number 9. Wayne's friend says, "Why don't you just wear two 9s?" That's how Wayne gets the number 99.

Wayne's hero, Gordie Howe, wore Number 9. Wayne wears Number 9 to honour his hero.

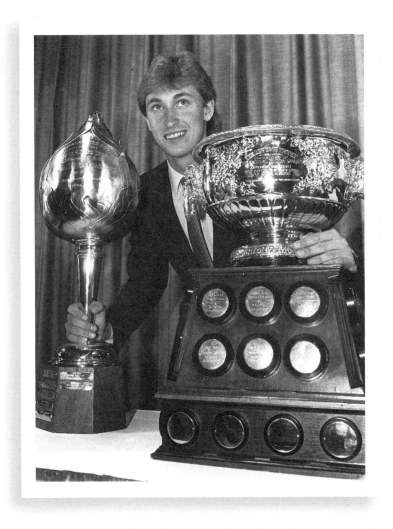

Wayne wins the Art Ross trophy for the most points.
June 9, 1981.

The NHL and Number 99

Wayne starts playing in the NHL in 1979. He plays for the Edmonton Oilers. In his first NHL season, Wayne shows fans how good he is. Wayne ties for the NHL scoring title. In his second season, Wayne wins the scoring title.

Wayne plays for the Edmonton Oilers for nine seasons: 1979–80 to 1987–88.

Wayne cheers after he breaks a record.

The Great One

In his third NHL season, Wayne
breaks a big record. Two players share
the record. They have scored 50 goals
in 50 games. It is an amazing record.
Wayne scores 50 goals in 39 games.
He shocks the hockey world.

Mike
Bossy and
Maurice Richard
both scored
50 goals in
50 games.

Wayne scored his 92nd goal with this puck.

The Great One

Wayne's third season takes him into another world. He scores 92 goals. That is 16 more than anyone has ever scored in one NHL season. He also gets 120 assists. Wayne gets 212 points in total.

Wayne says, "I was always taught that an assist is equal to a goal."

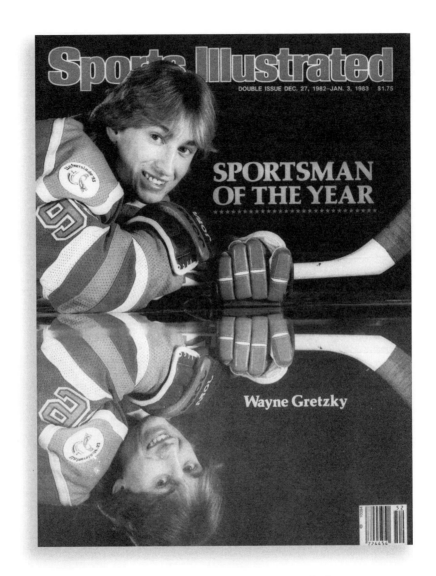

Wayne is the 1982 Sportsman of the Year.

The Great One

Wayne keeps scoring at an amazing pace. By the end of the 1982–83 season, Wayne is the best NHL player. He gets 709 points in his first four years with the NHL. Fans call Wayne "The Great One."

Wayne averages 203 points per season in his six best years. He is the only NHL player to score 200 points or more per year.

Wayne Gretzky, 1984.

The Stanley Cup

Some fans say: "Wayne has not won the Stanley Cup. How can he be the best player?" In 1983, Wayne becomes team captain. Wayne says: "We have one goal and one goal only. And that's to win the Stanley Cup."

Wayne screams with joy.

The Stanley Cup

Wayne learns how to win the Stanley Cup. The Oilers learn how to body check better. They spend more time on the ice. They spend less time in the penalty box. The Oilers win four Stanley Cups in five years.

Janet and Wayne wave to his fans.

Joy and Sorrow

Wayne marries Janet Jones on July 16, 1988. The wedding is in Edmonton. People call it Canada's royal wedding. It is a day of joy for hockey fans. One month later, the fans' joy turns to **sorrow**.

Wayne Gretzky and Peter Pocklington
talk about "The Trade."

Joy and Sorrow

August 9, 1988, is a sad day for
Edmonton. Wayne Gretzky is no
longer an Edmonton Oiler. Wayne is
traded. People call this "The Trade."
Hockey fans in Edmonton lose the
best hockey player of all time.

Wayne Gretzky is sold to the Los Angeles Kings for $18 million.

Wayne's fans wish him happy birthday.

Joy and Sorrow

Edmonton loves hockey. The fans love Wayne. They feel hurt and angry about the trade. "The Trade" is like watching a family member leave home. The mayor says, "It's like ripping the heart out of the city."

Wayne waves to his fans after his last NHL game.
April 15, 1999.

Later Years

Wayne leaves Edmonton. He plays for three other NHL teams. He retires in 1999. Wayne scores 2,857 points in the NHL. That is nearly 1,000 points more than anyone else.

The NHL retires Wayne's jersey number, 99. No other NHL player will ever be able to wear 99.

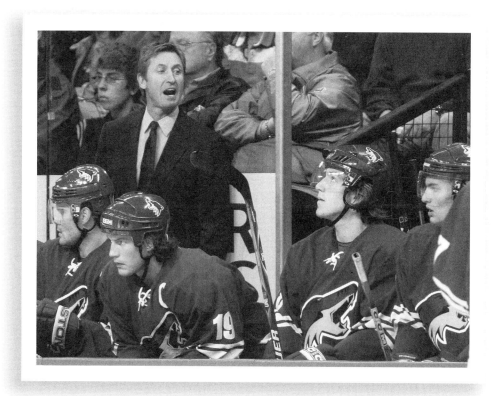

Wayne coaches the Phoenix Coyotes.
September 17, 2006.

Later Years

Today, Wayne works in the NHL as an owner and coach. His love of hockey remains strong.

Fans wonder if the "Next One" will break Wayne's point total of 2,857. It will never happen. "The Great One" will keep this record for all time.

Wayne Gretzky holds over 60 NHL records.

Glossary

league: an association of sports teams.

rare: very uncommon.

sorrow: sadness caused by loss.

Talking About the Book

What did you learn about Wayne Gretzky?

Why do you think the rules were bent
to allow Wayne to play hockey at the age
of six?

Why do you think Wayne was traded to
Los Angeles?

How do you think Wayne felt about
retiring in 1999?

What do the words "The Next One" mean?

The author says that Wayne will keep the
point total of 2,857 for all time. Do you
agree? Why or why not?

Picture Credits

Front cover photos (center photo): Robert Shaver/Hockey Hall of Fame (small photo): © CP. **Contents page** (top right): © Hockey Hall of Fame. (bottom left): © CP/Fred Chartrand. (bottom right): © Robert Shaver/Hockey Hall of Fame. **Page 4:** © CP/ Richard Lam. **Page 6:** © Robert Shaver/Hockey Hall of Fame. **Page 8:** © AP. **Page 10:** © Graphic Artists/Hockey Hall of Fame. **Page 12:** © Hockey Hall of Fame. **Page 14:** © CP/Brantford Expositor. **Page 16:** © Dennis Robinson/The Globe and Mail. **Page 18:** © Harry McLorinan/The Globe and Mail. **Page 20:** © Hockey Hall of Fame. **Page 22:** © Robert Shaver/Hockey Hall of Fame **Page 24:** © CP/Ron Poling. **Page 26:** © Robert Shaver/Hockey Hall of Fame. **Page 28:** © Matt Murnaghan/Hockey Hall of Fame. **Page 30:** © CP. **Page 32:** © CP. **Page 34:** © CP. **Page 36:** © CP/Ron Bull. **Page 38:** © CP/Ray Giguere. **Page 40:** © London Life-Portnoy/Hockey Hall of Fame, **Page 42:** © CP/Fred Chartrand. **Page 44:** © CP/John Woods.